AF323702

The Ferris Wheel

Poems By

Anthony Stachurski

ISBN: 0-9645034-0-9

Printed in the United States of America

FIRST PRINTING

TABLE OF CONTENTS

For Elizabeth

Broken Glass

I remember
Holding broken glass
To the sun
As a boy
Just for fun.
I made the world
Look cherry-pop bright.
I made a lie
Somehow
Seem right.

The Hustler

"Psst! Hey Buddy! Over here!"
From an alley dimly lit, a sleazy smile.
"You wanna buy?"
Dramatically, He opened up His overcoat
As if exposing Himself.

Pinned in rows:
A hundred watches ticked - off time;
The pearls, He claimed, were tiny moons,
The diamonds, distant stars.
All gold, of course, was from the sun
And guaranteed.

I waved my money clip in front of Him.
"Reveal one truth, instead, to help me
Through this world, one truth to stand
My hair on end and make me roll in ecstasy
Upon the ground."

He buttoned up His coat.
"Aach! Crazy talk," and shuffled off,
Looking back just once to shout,
"Don't make no trouble, eh!"

November

Day waits and listens in the rain
To the rattle of loose, unfastened things,
A stoplight's reckless swing
That rims the ends of empty streets,
As Time, blown up against a fence
Beside old papers, an unlaced shoe,
Watches the playground horse and train
Race madly nowhere in the mud
As every hole beneath a swing
Fills slowly up.

The houses sleep.
Lamplight on a wall.
Crayons on the floor, forgotten.
A stranger clicks brief echoes down a street.
Someone shuts a distant door.
The day's last voices drizzle
In an early dream that wind abandons
And cold.

The Ferris Wheel

From some carnival lot, the galaxy reels,
Cast off long ago like an old ferris wheel,

Axle-sheared, its dusty star-bulbs blinking around
Like the tired carousel of the spheres. Up and down,

Only stopping to drop the dead off
As we rock in our hard, wooden chairs at the top,

Watching, in fear, the whole void below,
Straining our eyes for the guardian angels aglow

The park entrance sign. Again, with a whoosh in our gut,
Passing planets and moons like saucers and cups

And comets whiplashing like wild roller coasters
Crowded with faces still horror struck. Stars

Everywhere like old Roman Candles fizzle away
As we turn from the darkness and pray,

Clutching each other, uneasy and cold,
Drifting deeper and darker into the unknown,

With blue cotton candy stuck in our hair,
The smell of stale popcorn still in the air.

The Picnic

Friends and relatives are doing
All the things you'd wanted them to do:
The women chatting as the men drink beer,
The children swinging from the apple tree
You'd planted long ago for times like these.
Yet, as you watch from the top porch step,
I think of Brueghel's "Wedding Dance,"
And that one man standing from the crowd,
Bringing all the world to view.

There's wine in the cellar now
And colored bottles on the windowsill,
But I recognize that look upon your face
As if you'd missed a step upon the stairs.
I see the worry in your eyes
This summer breeze lifting your old hair
Will never ease.

House Fire

I might have cried, "Holy! Holy!"
When the room flared with light,

But the drapes ignited,
The mirror went blind in a flash,
Wallpaper swans flocked to the air
As the roses blazed in the crystal glass.

Souls screamed in the couch
And writhed in the chairs.

They flayed in the floor
In sea-swells of fire and clung
To old throwrugs braided with death,
Or swirled around knot holes, down
To the cellar below.

Devils squeezed through the vents
And slammed shut the doors.

And I, too, was on fire, flaming away,
Waiting for angels to sound their bright horns

As my heart burned black as char,
As the house burned to the ground,
As the moon rose fuming with clouds
Across the infernal stars.

Side-View Mirror

Down the road at sixty-five, you never
Think you're going to die, pushing

Everything aside like roadside clover
That parts and bows behind you, so full

Of what's ahead you hardly ever check
The side-view mirror (except to pass)

To see the birds sucked in the glass,
The towns knocked flat, the clouds

Dragged down the corner of its eye,
The way one thing after another falls

Into that crystal ball.

The Answer

The answer is too clear,
As if in studying the moon
It had suddenly moved closer
To the window, and I could
See the dark plains now,
The craters and the rills.
I asked the question years ago-
It is an ancient one-
And I have been slow to answer,
Have been avoiding it.
Now, for some reason,
An answer is demanded, like
Being told sharply and
For the last time, to speak
Loudly and stand up straight.
And it bothers me to think
I had deceived myself, and I had,
Or that I hadn't really known
The answer, that I was shifting
Again, from leg to leg.

Winter Scene

Ponds stare at the sky
Like the eyes of dead fish.
Red Dogwood stains the snow
Like frozen blood.
The creek is twisted into ice.
The marsh - in ruins again.

Soon the night will shift
Its spotted turtle's back.
The Crab will crawl
Across the starry-gravelled sky.
The ground will stir again
With the tiny plants of ants.
Come spring the earth
Will bear her jelly mass,
Scattering leaves and stars overhead
With a tail's wag,
As if that was that.

Frozen silence now.
Only the Ironwoods speak when they sway,
Bending and groaning in the North Wind
Like the slow grinding of teeth.

The Black Hat

Hardly the room, what with hippos
And zebras swishing tails in our
Face, and fidgety rabbits and
Pigeons flying all over the place.
Yet, we kept our spirits up, grateful
For the sudden breeze and extra room
When the lid flipped up as He grabbed
One of us and we moved up the line,
All the while waiting, wondering who
We would be the next time around.
"It was fun," said a dog, "but it happened
Too fast," though a cow and a deer both
Started to cry without knowing why.
We just had to wait in the dark with
The stench and the sweat, unsure when
That giant thumbnail would swish like
A scythe overhead and hand-yank us up
To the gasps and guffaws, the small
Rounds of applause I suppose made Him
Smile and made it worthwhile.

Soldiers

On cold, fall days,
When the park was closed,
And the trees
Had dropped their leaves,
He'd come,
A stick held to his shoulder
Like a gun.
He'd march for hours
In the baggy suit
That flapped like a flag
Across his back until
He'd stop
To cock his head, like a dog,
And talk to God.
Sometimes he'd beat
The ground with his gun,
Or sit on the grass and cry.
Sometimes he'd just talk
On the phone to his brother
Who had died.

The Waiting Room

Sitting in a room
In the quiet air,
You listen to the world
Whirring in your ear,
And breathing slowly
Make it disappear.
Quiet now, aware,
You wait inside your self
Like someone staring
At a t.v. screen
After the flag's waved
And the anthem's sung
And the world's gone
Off the air.

And you wait
For the bliss that never comes,
Only to return
To the traffic's noise,
Again, without the joy
That was missing.

The Negative

Of all the photographs from Cedar Point,
I liked the one that showed my children
Tanned and laughing,
Piloting their rockets into space.
But when the negative fell out,
I held it to the light to see that day
Turned into night,
My children's hair so white and skin so gray,
Their eyes so frightened now and glazed,
They seemed like spirits in some afterlife,
Lost and dazed.
Something to myself I could not say,
Half rushing to their rooms to kiss them,
Half making sure into that night
Their little ships had not yet slipped away.

Potato Soul

One last chance
    I said,
Feeling my way
    Down the cellar stairs
To find my soul
    Tossed weeping mad
In a paper bag
    Some time ago
Because it didn't do the job,
    And now, once found,
With pity lifted up.
    How sadly changed:
Dirty, pulpy, wrinkled
    To the touch,
Sticking out a few small shoots
    Like the fins
Of some protesting fish,
    Or as if
This silly thing
    Had sprouted wings
And meant to fly away
    To demonstrate a grudge.
It stares at me
    From sad, indented eyes
As I wash and dry it up
    With hardly a splutter and sputt,
Seeing all the rotten spots
    And last gray drops
Of putrid blood,
    Too late for salt or love.

Memorial Day Parade

But as the band
Marched over the hill,
The snare drums rolled
Like sudden rounds of rifle fire;
Batons flashed and fell
Like swords out of the trees;
Cymbals clashed like bombs;
Bass drums boomed like distant guns.

Then the music died
Like a wounded carousel
As one by one our soldiers
Fell into a heap.

And the people slowly turned away
In grief.

Winter Lines

All day the highway trembled in my hands
Past towns and farms and cattle
Standing in a trance.
Cold winds rammed the car and shrieked
In the crack the window made.

And as the sun went down,
Images remained like fingerprints
Upon the dash:
That small boy sledding down the lawn, alone,
That couple fighting in the car,
The frozen animals along the road
Like toys upturned upon the floor.

And then a mood came over me
As if my heart were setting too, and birds
Were flying to my branches for the night.
And I, across the darkened land, had now become
The soulful moon.

The Fall

He woke
From a troubled sleep
As fruit blew down
Upon the ground
Like footsteps fleeing.
He shuddered
In the first cold wind
He'd ever known
And snuggled up to Eve.
He thought it strange
The beasts had left
Without a sound
As he listened
To the wind and watched
The dark clouds
Tamper with the moon.

Box Elders

They gather in the evenings
Down by the river, off to themselves,
Huddled in the mud
As fireflies swirl about their heads
Like sparks from an oildrum fire.
Half-hidden in the smoky mist
Of cigarettes, they stand in fixed
Gesticulation, tired and drunk, unshaven,
Propped against some cable wire
As on a flophouse line, fallen
In the ditch face down, or cradled
In each others' burly arms.
Broad-leaved shoulders hunched
Against the rain,
They hope to stay the night
And not be asked to move along again.

Man in the Mirror

Like a Time-Life scene
Depicting man's ascendancy from ape,
He steps out of the misty past, pushing
The leaf-green shower curtain back
Like some giant fern wet with dew.
He towels dry, then lopes toward the sink
And leans into the folding mirrors
To wipe a clearing in the steam.
He saw the metaphor last year, and now,
When in a certain frame of mind,
He tilts the mirrors in until he sees himself
Repeated in the glass, blurred backwards
To the past.
He waves and they wave back.
He asks them questions.
"You there, number ten. Could you please speak
Upon the origin of man?"
He fidgets and looks aside.
"Then, twenty-four, tell us what you know
About the soul."
He stares back at the man as if he'd been
The one who'd asked.
"Well, what about it thirty-two?
What the hell is wrong with all of you?"
A hundred faces curve away in confusion and dismay
As the man adjusts the mirror back to number one
And the bathtub drain clunks shut
As if the game was done.

Resolution

When your feet first
Touch the cold
Tile floor, when
The children start
The morning with
Their shouts,

It's always harder
Than you thought,

The way each
Day begins where
All your life left off
And gravity renews
Its old hold

On you.

Heavenly Invitation

Last night a great, white cloud arose
Into a shining palace, with stars
Strung out across the sky like party lights,
And the moon hung high in every tree.
Planets bobbed like bright balloons,
And comets popped like champagne corks
Into infinity
As God unrolled the Milky Way up to my door.

But, no! I'd seen this before:
Gas and dust, the clever use of props,
Inevitably, a fit, too much to drink,
Perhaps someone forgot to bow.
And then the sky upturned, the Dippers hurled,
Galaxies tossed whizzing through the air,
The sun, come dawn, gutting it all.

Night Drive

The city drifts away
Like a galaxy in space.

Car lights fade
Like a comet's thinning tail.

I pass the minor constellations
Of a hundred main-street towns

And service station signs that rise
Like vacant moons above the tree-top line.

A beacon pulses red
Like one last dying star

And then it's dark and cold.
I may be lost.
A mist upon the road
I slow and roll the window partly down.

The stars beneath my wheels
Crackle like leaves.

Street Talk

You just can't hide
The basketball hoops
That droop from each garage,
Or the ten-speeds dying
On the front porch steps
Gasping for breath. No way
To keep the mailboxes off booze
Or stop the angry weeds
From pushing up the drive.
No use to think the garbage cans
Won't roll away one day
And spill the truth.

Man in the Jar

Somewhere by the Dead Sea,
Or Nag Hammadi,
I had stood on a village street
And shouted: "The world was a mistake!"

That was my premise,
The reason I hid
In the skull-colored hills
Beneath God's burning eye
And all the angry mob of stars
Beneath the sentried moon
Pretending sleep,

Far from angels' eyes
And archon ears
And fools shouting for my head.

In a hole, in a jar,
My tongue scrolled tightly
In my mouth, I waited
For the farmer's plow,
The shepherd's arcing stone,

When I awoke
To the moon's face peering
Through the drapes
And voices stirring in the street
Like dust.

Halloween

They mock themselves tonight: hags on brooms
Whisking through the living room (But how to stop them?);
Bedsheet ghosts floating down the halls (Not yet, Oh God, not yet!);
Convicts dragging ball and chain along the floors;
And howling monsters smeared with blood (It's only paste!).
Yet, not to spoil their fun, we help to make them up.

Outside, the night's black cape swirls 'round the sky
But keeps its one good eye, the moon, exposed,
Delighted when the leaves attack like swarms of bats
And wicked limbs reach out to snatch them in.

Our children rush into a night
We little understand,
Where evil forces rule the world and cut them up
Like gruesome pumpkins burning on the ledge,
Then laugh, as on the street they smash their heads
To celebrate this harvest of the dead.

"That the sons of God
saw the daughters of men,
that they were fair."
                    Gen. 6:2

The Sons of God

Tall and handsome
With their silver chains
And silk, white shirts,
Our fathers trespassed on the earth,
Laughing, swearing, drinking beer,
Tossing empties in the air.
They spied our mothers peering
From the woods
And screwed them,
Roaring back into the sky
To hide
As our mothers cried
And felt their bellies swelling
Like the moon.

One summer night it seemed
I heard somebody knocking softly
At the door, then saw this old man
Shining through the screen.

But it was just a dream.

Dry Dock

Up and down the asphalted canals,
Trailers slump in the mid-day sun
Like rows of pleasure boats outworn,
Moored by utility lines now.
Heat waves lap against the sides, bobbing
The cans and bottles half-buried in the mud,
Swaying the unmowed grass like reeds
As the road, in buckled swells, rolls out
Towards the dry and vacant fields.

Open windows hang upon the walls
Like paintings of a blue and shining sea;
Lacy curtains ebb and flow against the screens
As dreamers dream.

Then: a tug on the line,
knocks and creaks,
rose vines snap, a sudden bow,

The scent of White Alyssum breaking on the prow.

No Exit

It's strange.
You didn't get an invitation.
In fact, it seems you've always been here
Studying the tapestries of ancient ruins
And silk-stitched comets dooming earth.
What, with the food and games, the girls,
You just forget.
But now you're curious and ask to go.
You ask the maitre d' to get your coat.
He won't. He offers you another drink instead,
Drinking it himself when you refuse.
You go to leave but can't locate the door.
There are no doors or windows, only walls
And ceilings and floors.
You laugh. Some kind of joke.
You think you might be on the "Candid Camera" show.
But no. You want to ask another fellow there,
But that would be embarrassing.
And then again, you'd spread alarm.
And you can see he knows, the way he scans
The room each time he tilts his head to laugh.
You want to shout, "Walls! Walls! Run for your lives!"
But what could you do, find a wall extinguisher
And break the glass, set up the door
And walk through?

Desert Queen

She sleeps outstretched in sheer moonlight
Beneath the dim tiara of the sky, her crown.
Nearby, a dozen motel towns like campfires burn
As shotguns boom across the dunes.

The tall saguaros love her so
And guard her loyally, though old, demented,
Stupefied with gin, too drunk to even flay
The bats away.

Now tiremarks scar the land.
Broken bottles glint like fallen stars
Along the trail.
Coyotes prowl among the gray bouquets
Of prickly pear, and owls,
As if down halls and out of broken doors,
Glide and disappear
Over the rubble of early morning clouds.

Nightwatch

The dog is making strange noises;
Cerberus is dreaming,
Banging the wall with his tail.

Yes - dog, wife and me.
Now I remember, sitting up
At the edge of the bed and rubbing my eyes,
Lifting the shade on a world dimly lit
By some back-alley moon,
Looking outside for strange lights
In the sky, a bush bursting in flames,
But only the neighborhood drunk guided home
By the dull, pointless stars
Of the city's side streets,
Or a man, at the window like me
Looking out, holding his head like
A small, frightened moon as he weeps.

I pull down the shade
And kiss my wife on the cheek
As I lie back in bed.
The glare of the clock, like a no-exit sign,
Casts the room in a lurid, red haze.
The dog, by my side, trembles at times
Breathing long, human sighs
In his sleep.

Creature From the Black Lagoon

We sat there in the dark those Sunday afternoons
Waiting for the light to break upon the screen,
The way each day's first sunbeams strike the earth,
Then counted, all aloud, the numbers
As they crackled down towards the zero of creation.

The sound track scrambled out its eerie theme
As credits listed all the characters
Whose names appeared to us one and the same.
And then the trawler gurgled on the scene delivering
The dark-haired beauty sunning on the bow.

We watched the plot unfold,
Though, sometimes, perhaps the focus wasn't right,
We'd turn to the projection room to see emerge
Through swampy, layered mists of rank, tobacco smoke,
A giant Shadow on the wall.
A fierce and ugly face appeared as if He were the Creature
Looking out to view Himself, illuminated
In the way a kid at night will hold a flashlight
To his face to scare someone.

It seemed as if the light were coming out of Him -
Sun rays from a fearsome God -
As if the light were passing through His mind, a prism
Spreading out the heroes, villians, spies and beauties,
Supernumeraries only there to die.

Amidst the swaying strands of kelp, He treaded,
Gulping murky water through His mouth and out
His blood-red gills, His eyes like silver lures watching
As the anchor grinned into the muck.

And then the slimy hand fin clasped her shapely foot.
She screamed and fainted, fluttered like a ribbon
Pinned to Him as they descended to His lair
Where lovingly He stared at her and stroked her hair.

Above, the frantic search began, and then the capture,
Deaths, escapes, the entire town in fear,
And all the while within the movie room, we heard
Excited shuffling, as if He loved the boos and screams,
The feel of flattened popcorn boxes slashing at the screen.

And then:
Police cars lined the beach,
The sky snarled back displaying
Its array of teeth
As we leaned forward in our seats.

At last He staggered forth returning to the sea
For oxygen, His love limp in His arms,
Her dress amiss and torn, her breasts almost revealed.
Too weak to hold her anymore, He laid her gently down
And struggled on toward the water's edge
As bullets drilled Him (dead, we thought)
Into the deep.

The End.
The eerie theme song played again
As we moved up the aisle into the mezzanine
Afraid we'd see Him green and bleeding
Stumbling down the stairs.

Then squinting as the exit doors were opened wide,
We blocked the sunlight with our hands
And ran for home,
That Sunday afternoon
We saw *The Creature From the Black Lagoon.*

The Fourth of July

They labored through the last of light,
Leaving cows to the darkened barns
And dishes in the sink,
Then piled the kids in pick-up trucks
And drove the furrows up on Fuller's Field
To park in rows like at the drive-in show.
Soon beer cans squirted in the air
And husbands slipped their hands beneath
The dresses of their wives.
The children laughed as German Shepherds
Humped somebody pinned against the cab.
The women happy that everyone was happy.
Then fireworks shinnied up the sky and boomed,
Spraying red and blue and silver sparks
More beautiful than stars.
And, for a while, the world seemed made for man.
But then it rained.
Engines groaned in the heavy air.
Headlights flashed and fizzled down the hills
Into the corn
Like one last rocket's flare.

Dark Hours

I wake. It's 3 a.m.

No moon, again.

The cold mainspring
Of night wound down,
The stars have stopped
Their ticking.

A rafter snaps.

Snow shifts and slips
On the roof like a man
Repeatedly losing his grip.

A small, pitiful voice
From the reservoir tank
Cries out down the hall.

The water pipes shake
In a fit.

The earth trembles
Over the basin of time

And drips.

Man at the Window

"Speak! Speak!," he shouted mentally.
But what did he expect to see,
An angel hovering at the fourteenth floor?
"Look Bob. It's like this..."
Or a Cessna hauling a trailer sign:
"ALL MYSTERIES SOLVED. CALL 629-4681.
         ASK FOR GOD."

Small clouds hung above the city
Like the white balloons of a comic book
Devoid of words or plot

As with sadness he recalled, how, seven years ago today,
While watching *Lost Horizon* on t.v., his wife
Had stood at the kitchen door and told him
That Hans Adolph Krebs had passed away.

"Life, life, life, life, flife, flife, falife...,"
Or, "World, world, world, world, dworld, dworld, dawirl...,"
He'd repeat a different word each day
Until the meaning went away, a practice
Just to ground himself, he'd say.

Or he'd invent a little rhyme:

        Wizards leap as lizards weep.
        Time passes by with a whiz.
        The world's a foot too fat to fit.
        And nobody knows what is.

Sometimes he'd try to voice a poem:
"This cold wind in my soul...,"
"This pain that grows...,"
"This emptiness of air..."

Or, sometimes, like now,
He'd just stand there
And stare.

Men on the Beach

Conch shells jut from the beach
Like old men's ears.

Driftwood twitches in the breeze,
Lifting the thin, gray hairs of seaweed
From their shoulders.

And every wave
Slips glittering away
The fortunes at their feet.

All day the wrinkled caves suck
At the shore and drool down
The corners of their vowelled mouths

As the dolphins leap
With their curious smiles
Out of the blue, insatiable sea.

Reflections on "Ten Sucked From Jet"

Tanned and happy,
Wearing blue Hawaiian shirts,
Looking down upon the beauty of the clouds,
That is, before the door blew out.
No time now for Sharon Cross to join the P.T.A.,
For Robert Diehl to coach the Little League.

And on the way towards the grave,
Did some hold hands and sing, *Amazing Grace?*
Or did they raise their middle finger to the sky,
Feeling betrayed that the sky was much too blue
To die that day, that not one guardian angel
Showed its face.
Did others treat the whole affair as comic and absurd?
Computing rates of free-falling bodies,
Performing swan dives as they plummeted through air.

Who knows?
I turned the page to get away from all this tragedy
Only to read: "Gargoyle Falls, Kills Nun on Street Below."
And then, "Father of Five Drowns in Septic Tank in Idaho."

I Dream of Truth

I am walking away from a castle of faith,
Down a winding, dirt road into the woods,
Seeking truth, real truth.

But it's more like a jungle.
The trees are tall and slimy and tangled
In vines. The roots are exposed like mangroves
And resemble huge bird cages.
It's dark. I can't see the sun for the leaves.
And soon I'm lost and confused.

I spy a book: A Spiegel catalogue,
Wet and soiled, and thumb hurriedly
Through the dog-eared pages of models
Wearing swimsuits and panties and bras.
Someone has drawn a penis in a woman's mouth.
Then luggage and sweaters and shoes etc.
On one page is written: "For the absolute truth
Turn to page 115." I do.
"Now turn to page 145," it says. I do.
"Now turn to page 182."

And I do.

Blue Angels

As homebound traffic thins,
We take our lanes and race along
The open highway leading to the sky,
So blue and wide...

And then, Blue Angels, we,
Climbing bridges to the clouds,
      sliding down
Like otters in the blue jet stream,
Passing, banking, looping cloverleafs,
Booming down the skyway, contrails billowing
Like clouds of dust until
We soar into the last of light,
So close our souls might touch,
And for a shining moment lost until
From out our diamond fountainhead we burst
Above the grandstand's final cheer, disappearing
In the dusky corners of the sky where
Streetlights mark the landing strips
Blue men touch down each night.

The Mad House

"Who is brave enough? Or mad enough?
For you will scream in terror and beg for release.
You sir. Step right up," the barker cried.
I laughed at the arrow stuck in his head
And the bloodshot eyes that flayed on springs,
The crazy, gizmo sounds and graphics on the walls,
The rubber mouth that puked the patrons out.

"What the hell," I said, and went inside,
Adjusting to the dim, red light and screams
Of freak-show mannequins, the world gone strange.
The room that spun - until I staggered out;
The crazy looking glass;
The room upturned with chairs and tables nailed
Above me to the floor; and in the hall of mirrors, lost!
And then no door!
And in the dark, the skeleton that talked:
"Please, walk this way!"
Until the floor gave out, and I slid down
A slimy tongue into a grave.

I wiped my brow and smiled to show I was O.K.
Then sat upon a bench to rest.
A clown walked by, but on his hands, and asked
What I was doing upside down.
A sudden migraine caused the world to spin,
And what, with all the people screaming, shouting,
Lost, confused, the evening sky becoming dim and red,
I left.

That night, a phone call from my doctor woke me
From my sleep. "Look, Tony. I've got bad news for you.
The x-rays show you've only got five days to live."
"Oh, great!" I cried. "But that's not all," he said,
"I've been trying to reach you all this week."

Waiting for George Burns

I wait for His telephone call
And watch for Him on the six o'clock news,
Or sit by the radio like an R.C.A. dog
And listen for the sound of the Master's voice.

I check out the bookstores and bus depots,
Attend midnight mass in old, city churches,
Scan every diner and telephone booth
For white-haired, old men wearing sweaters
And glasses.

Twice, I was sure it was Him:
Once at the burlesque show sitting in the front row,
And then in a marathon, some months ago;
I called out, but He never looked back.

Anyway, one day, I'm told
He'll be there in the mirror
Standing beside me as I'm combing my hair,
Or at the edge of my bed
When I wake in the night, upset or scared,
When I'm sick of waiting, out
Walking the streets,
There He will be, perhaps on a bench,
Tapping His feet,
Smoking His smelly cigar,
Impatiently waiting for me.

The Homeland

My father had always wanted me
To see his homeland
And hear about his past,
Understand the life he'd lived.
I showed no interest then,
So he shut his mouth.
Now he is old and dying,
So I dream a lot
Of carrying him back
To his village
To see his house and garden plot,
His church and school, his desk
Beside the window,
His best friend's house,
The candy shop.
And when he tires
And wants to stop,
I merely hoist him higher up.
Even on the night
His head slumped on my chest,
As was my duty as a son,
On and on I ran more quickly
Down the streets
Holding out his arm and shouting:
"Show me! Show me!"

The Insane Asylum

He stands at the door with poop in his pants
Speaking in moontalk, I'm told; and yet,
I understand him. "Atma ca tal," he says:
"Life is hell."

The place is huge. It has to be; everyone's here:
Bob Johnson from Detroit, Dennis Lang from Flint
(The last I'd heard he was doing well),
Sue Stevens (Susy, you too?). Oh, Hello, Mrs. Gordon,
Mrs. Gordon! Mrs. Gordon!
Suddenly, a man with one leg shouts: "Why,
Why is there anything at all?"
Another man, respected for his research
On the origins of bellybutton lint, replies:
"So green horses can pee-pee in their pants."
Everyone laughs and stomps his feet.
A man with a dart in his head now asks:
"Why were we put here on this Earth?"
A former nun replies: "To rub a little mustard
On our legs." The place goes nuts.
They smash the windows and the doors.
They do the wave.
"My turn," a naked woman asks. "Who made God?"
A precocious boy stands up and shouts: "The Blob."
They jump out windows, they piss in the air,
They eat each other's underwear.
But soon the mania stops.
Soon, many are crying. Others begin masturbating.
Still others have gathered in groups to practice
Extinct bird calls.
And then the drone of voices again, like
Congregational prayer.

Snowfall in July

Alone he stands
With sled in hand,
Waiting on the hill,
Staring out
His glass-domed world
At plastic pines
And porcelain deer
That graze on dusty
Dimestore shelves,
At pennants tacked
To sky-blue walls
And ceiling bulbs
Like suns commanded
Still.

Spiritual Reminders

It's strange they don't annoy me,
But still I like to see the nuns and priests
Out on the street.
I say, "Hello, Father," or
"Good morning, Sister," even though
I know from reading in the news
They're only human, too.
I respect them anyway
For their attempt "to know, to serve,
And to love God."
And that extends to holy people everywhere.
If I see Hindus at the store, I smile
And say, "Hari Govinda," or simply, "OM."
They're all reminders to me
That I may be wrong,
That there is a purpose to life,
That in the end we just don't die
Or go mad.

But I don't think so.

Center for the Leader Dogs
for the Blind

Behind a row of evergreens:
Backyard apple trees and sidewalks
Lined with daffodils and red park benches,
A white gazebo for the charm,
And German Shepherds sitting on the lawn
Like luggage waiting to be claimed.

Then outstretched arms and white canes tapping,
Black sunglasses, just a game of pin-the-tail
On anything at all.
Or victims of some terrible experiment gone wrong.
Each few steps they stop to cock their heads
As if they stood at the edge of the world
And now could hear above the songs of morning birds
Loose gravel sliding.
Then back and forth along the pathways

To endure
The branches' teary lash,
The pardon-me collisions with the trash,
The sight of blossoms blowing in the wind,
But of some other spring.

A Reconsideration of
"That Holy Night"

O.K. So maybe the clouds weren't "angels,"
And stars weren't "vigil lights,"
Or airvents "dervishes that whirled in ecstasy
Throughout the night."
So maybe I don't have a soul.
And I admit that in that moonlight "pure and tender,"
I saw a fish float belly up
And packs of rats inside the trash,
That it's just poetry to write, "a bridge at prayer,
Its rosary of lights upraised in decades to the shore,"
An outright lie to say, "I knelt before the altar of the sky
And took the moon into my mouth,"
And that for all I know
As "lightning bolts shut heaven's door,"
I'd only wished it so.

Nightwalk

Tonight I walk the ends of ways,
Howling like the wind that rushes
Black and angry clouds
Across my inner eye, the moon.
And all the shadows of my thoughts
Make hordes of monsters on the walls.
There's no one out but me
And one curled leaf, my heart, scraping
Down the street.
Tonight, my soul just doesn't care
And seeks the end of light,
Tramps the darkest distance to itself
All night.

"I like trees because they seem
more resigned to the way they
have to live than other things do."
Willa Cather

Scene at a Maximum Security Camp
for Trees

Behind bars of morning shadows
Trees stood quietly at toil.
In former lives these men and women
Had been atheists, and now were doing time
Producing food and oxygen, holding down the soil.

And every day, they waited
As the sun dozed off at noon.
"Keys! Keys!" the Jays would scream
As cell doors opened wide.
But the Maple Trees had snatched them in.
Then winds rushed in to frisk the trees;
A riot would begin.
The Oaks shot acorns in the air.
The Pine trees lobbed grenades.
Willows lashed out at the sky, blinding
The fat-assed warden's eye.
In mob delirium they bent and strained to run
Who could not even walk.
They cracked and snapped. They bled
And toppled over dead, trembling down, undone,
As the bloodied sun smeared its cuts across the sky
And swung their shadows shut behind them once again.

All night the owls patrolled the woods,
For no trees slept as the moonlight scanned them
And the rats gnawed at their feet,
As they stood, whispering of mythical escapes
And free love, while acting as windbreaks,
Purifying the air, and aiding in the prevention
Of floods.

Sea World

You do a hundred tricks each day
To please the crowds,
Then shinny up on stage to smile
And kiss my face.

But, lately, the last performance through,
I've watched you rub along the glass retainer wall
In orbit like some asteroid restrained
From deep and starry space.

And now, tonight,
I spy your dark and heavy form listing
Like a shipwreck
On the bottom of the pool.

I dive to you and stroke your side.

You rise and undulate your cage
As I hold to you
Back and forth across your body drawn
As if I were a bow that played you
To a melancholy song.

Then suddenly you writhe with speed.
With every power stroke
The walls reverberate.

I fall aside and watch you rage
Until with final pounding fluke and bursting sound,
Spuming, arching, gleaming free,
The water weeping from your face,
Beneath the hoop of the man-in-the-moon

You leap.

Thoughts in a Fast-Food Diner

Look at us in worn-down heels
Shuffling down the line with acne
Rouge can't hide, or Clearasil.
And gray hairs squirming in the light.
That poor guy's coat,
The old man trying to find a seat
As french fries tumble off his tray.
Go ahead! Laugh! People suffer
Over stuff like this!
The way the waitress has to smile
And say: "What'll it be today, Honey?"
And you know her feet are killing her.
And she only calls you "Honey" for the money.

"God forbid!
A few loose threads and such a face!
At least the guy's got a coat to wear!
So he's too fat, and she's too thin.
So there's a little lettuce and tomato
On the floor. That's life!
And maybe the old lady thinks her gray hair
Looks distinguished!
Maybe the waitress likes to smile!
And hey! Maybe you are a "Honey!"

The Movie Show

I'm watching a gangster movie on t.v.
When the Bad Guy flicks his cigarette away
And says: "Hey wait! Just everybody wait!
What is this anyway? You? Me? This scenery?
Whose lines are these?"
The other actors look down at the floor
And slowly put their guns away, embarrassed
That they hadn't thought of this before.
The sexy blonde stops wiggling her butt
And throws her arms around her man. "Yeh,"
Supportively she states.
A prop slams down, making an empty sound.
"So what! I need the dough," a tough guy says
(who would be dead by now if the show hadn't
been delayed). "And what's the difference anyhow?"
They stop and turn my way.
"Hey you," the leader shouts. "You there on the couch
Stuffing popcorn in your mouth. Are you God?"
My beer can topples to the floor. I nearly choke.
"Me, God? Oh no! I'm just an actor, too, like you,
But in a different play. It's all mysterious
And strange."

The sun shines through the window lke a spotlight
On my face. The furniture seems too in place.
I switch the t.v. off to stop their bickering,
When, right on cue, the doorbell rings
To go backstage.

The Path

Watch for broken glass;
It may be dark.
The moon is seldom seen.
A rope might be a snake
Though the buzzards are real.
What can I say?

Be forewarned:
You were not meant to know a thing.
There may be chaos and nothingness,
Saints hanging from the trees.
So many truths are dark and mean,
Yet be prepared for ironies.

You may see angels selling lemonade;
They only know their names.
And you must learn things for yourselves
Or be set back again and again.

You know the rewards:
Pride, self-confidence, inner strength,
Truth.

Remember them, when it rains.

A Summer Scene

Inside a city street
A man sits on the front porch steps
And waters his lawn,
Staring at the rows of gabled roofs
As if they might be mountaintops.
He sups a beer
And smokes a cigarette
And watches clouds drift off.

Then suddenly he grinds
That cigarette beneath his feet
And flings the garden hose aside
To let it writhe against the house
And cry.

For the second time
The wife calls out:
"Come get your supper, John!"
And the children ask
Where Daddy's gone.

Heavenly Fear

Then what?
At first you might be thinking:
Flowers, jewels, blue skies every day.
"Hey, this is great!"
But, still, there would be questions
That should have been answered by now.
And all you'd gotten so far were grins
From some angel-faced wimps,
And the standard, brainless reply:
"God works in mysterious ways."
That would get you riled.
Soon there'd be meetings at the edge of town,
Far from the sound of perfunctory hymns,
Tough talk of truth, of melting down harps
For guns and knives.
But up on the soapbox, your fist in the air,
Really, what could you say:
"Take another God? Let us pray?"

Lady in White

She skits between the shadows,
Stopping here and there to watch
The world go strange,
Then falls upon the lawn,
Her white dress filthied now,
A toadstool suddenly upsprung
Without the rain.
Her red hair blazing
Near my frightened pines,
She grips the earth-go-round
As if it dizzied her,
Or through her paw-soft hands
She feels the world soon coming
To an end.
Then flits away
Through exits in the air
Toward the pale, omniscient moon.

Night Passage

Without the slightest tremble
From below
Or heave of steady swells,
The earth steams somewhere, listing.
A chill wind blows the smoke back
From the chimney stacks
As flags strain at the ropes and whip
The metal posts to ringing.
Night clouds rush like icebergs
Into the moonlight's scanning beam
As men stare out their cabin rooms
Upon a troubled wake of stars.

A Crying Time

There should be a designated time for crying,
Say, every Wednesday at 1:00,
When you could weep over your divorce,
Or your kid's leukemia, or the loss of your faith.
Everything would come to a halt that day
As soft, peaceful music played over the
Public address system.
And you could cry wherever you were at the time:
A priest in the confessional,
A kid in the garage, a bus driver at a stop.
And if someone felt self-conscious,
He could step inside a church, or in an alley,
Or pretend to read a newspaper, or if he were a janitor,
He could go into the broom closet and bang the pail
With the mop to cover up the sobs.
And then you'd dry your eyes and blow your nose
And answer the telephone,
Or smile at the person next to you
As you started the car back up.

Harp Music

The old woman sits
By the subway wall
And plays her harp.
We want to stop, but
Have a train to catch.
We toss our souls
Into her cap, then rush
Through the dark
To the hum of the track
Hanging by our straps.

Night Train

You neither take the window view
To lean out with the others when they say "Goodbye,"
The way that actors in the movies do,
Nor check the ticket for the time and place,
The spelling of your name; there's no mistake.
You sit and wait and watch the others move
Like apparitions in the glass.

And then the whistle shrieks.
The doors slam shut in echoes down the line.
The coaches jolt and creak.
The engine weeps along the track.
You stare ahead as loved ones pace beside you crying,
Reaching out their hands to you
Until the platform ends.

And then, around the bend,
The billboards laughing in the rain.

My Prayer

This morning, rising in the dark,
I feel like praying. I don't know why.
Maybe it was the dark clouds
And the empty streets.
I would kneel by the bed like a kid
Putting my hands together like you see
People doing in hallway pictures
Or over somebody's bed who was religious.
It's dumb and embarrassing in a way, though.
You wouldn't want your parents or wife
Or kids seeing you, as if it were an admission
Something was wrong, that you were unhappy.
But sometimes there is, and sometimes you are.
Besides I'm not even religious,
Not even sure that "there's got to be something."
But I think I'd like there to be -
To know, love and serve God.
Then again, I'm not sure.
Sometimes I dream I'm being tried in court.
A judge stands up directing me to prove
My faith in God by stepping over a line
Drawn on the floor. The jury glares at me
Then leans across the rail to watch my big toe
Barely touch the line. "That's not enough!" they cry.
I just don't know.
I remember seeing Isaac Asimov in a t.v. interview
When the reporter asked if he believed in God.
For a minute it was awkward: so many viewers watching,

The effect it might have, his reputation,
His own religious name.
But "No," he replied softly. And I always
Admired him for that.
So, I won't pray.
On mornings like this I'll just sit on the couch
And watch the sun come up or listen to the rain
And let the matter end that way.

The Magic Show

Older, thinner now, with coattails frayed,
He feigns His arm through Time and Space,
This last performance of the night.

Carnations bloom from His lapel
And diamonds trickle from His ears.
In thin air - Poof! - the sun is gone, while
In the other black-gloved hand appears the moon.

But then a world rolls down His sleeve
Onto the floor.
And as He whirls to gather it, we spot
The secret pockets sewn into the lining
Of His coat.
His top hat tips and lands upon its rim.
And from the false compartment lid, a rabbit
Skitters off to hide among the curtain folds.
A snake uncoils and hisses at the lights
As white doves whistle to the highest beams.

The music stops.
The curtain tries to close but jams halfway.
The spotlight turns away.
People faint and fall back in their chairs
While others kneel and pray,

As He stands like a statue in the rain,
Then vanishes backstage.

> "Who has no house now,
> will build him one no more."
>
> *Herbsttag (Autumn Day)*
> Rainer Maria Rilke

Homeless

What can I do, pretend?
Never!
But, still, it's true,
I'm like the man that Rilke warned about,
Who built no house,
And now must walk the streets
These autumn days no friend to God.

What people say of men like me is true
And yet insensitive,
For who would build a faith
With rotten wood?
What fool would pound one stick
Into the sinking ground?

No! Better to walk the streets
And live among the sparrows and the leaves
Even if it's cold and wet,
And lightning strikes like flashing teeth
About your naked feet.

Stood Up

It's raining.
But then
It's always raining.
The streetlamp
Makes a star of me
As if to spotlight
My stupidity.
I've stood upon
The corner now so long
My shadow's stuck
Into the wall.
My feet hurt.
I've got a chronic
Cold.
People snicker
As they pass
And yet I
Still look up
At every car
That splashes by
And listen
For those footsteps
Never slowing down
Behind me.

Last Rights

Lord, let me die
With my brass knuckles on,
Smacking my fist in my palm
All the way.
Help me keep my resolve
When that Bing Crosby voice
Calls my name from above,
And the sweetest, white angels
Escort me to God.
Then, eye to eye,
Pray my senses be straight,
My legs not give out
As I shout: "Lord! Two final sins!
One swift kick in Your ass!
One good smack on Your chin!"

About the Author

Anthony Stachurski is a Michigan poet who resides in Rochester Hills. He is a former high school and college teacher who now devotes himself to the writing of poetry.

His poems have appeared in *The Wayne Literary Review*, *The Detroit News*, *Writers' Digest*, *The Sandcutter*, *Arizona Review*, and other publications. The author's upcoming book will be a collection of love poems.